really easy piano

THE

COLLECTION

DISNEY ARTWORK TM AND © 2019 DISNEY
BACKGROUND IMAGE COURTESY OF ADOBE STOCK

ISBN: 978-1-5400-8390-6

Visit Hal Leonard Online at
www.halleonard.com

Contact us:
Hal Leonard
7777 West Bluemound Road
Milwaukee, WI 53213
Email: info@halleonard.com

In Europe, contact:
Hal Leonard Europe Limited
42 Wigmore Street
Marylebone, London, W1U 2RY
Email: info@halleonardeurope.com

In Australia, contact:
Hal Leonard Australia Pty. Ltd.
4 Lentara Court
Cheltenham, Victoria, 3192 Australia
Email: info@halleonard.com.au

THE FROZEN

COLLECTION

FROZEN

FROZEN 2

FROZEN

Do You Want to Build a Snowman?

Music and Lyrics by Kristen Anderson-Lopez and Robert Lopez

In the movie, this track shows Anna growing up and desperate to play with her older sister Elsa who, after accidentally hurting Anna with her power to control snow and ice, rarely leaves her room during their childhood. During the song, we can see Anna singing and intermittently knocking on Elsa's door as the movie fast-forwards through their upbringing, which includes the tragic death of their parents. It's during this time of mourning that an unhappy Anna knocks for the final time, asking "what are we gonna do?".

Hints & Tips: This should be played delicately. The melody line is made up of short phrases with rests in between. Make sure you count carefully and don't rush the eighth notes.

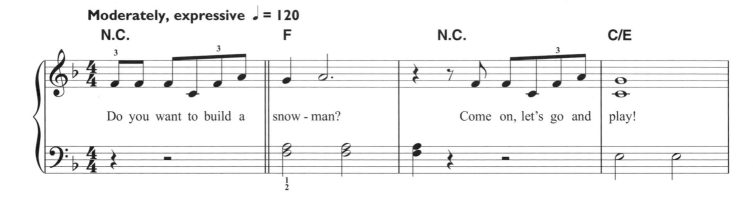

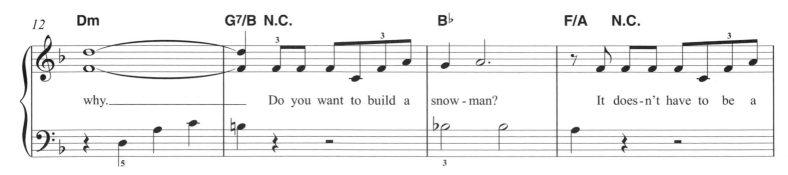

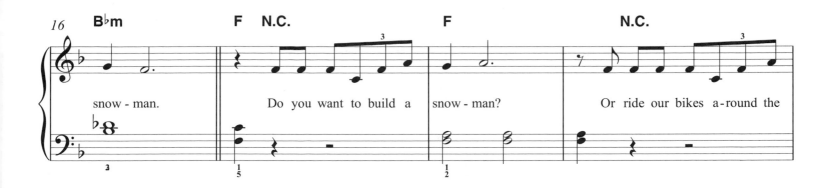

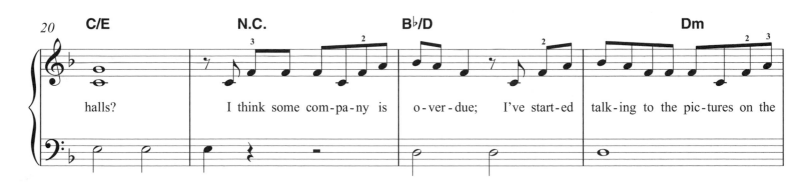

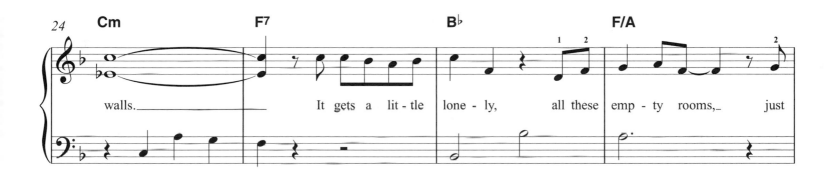

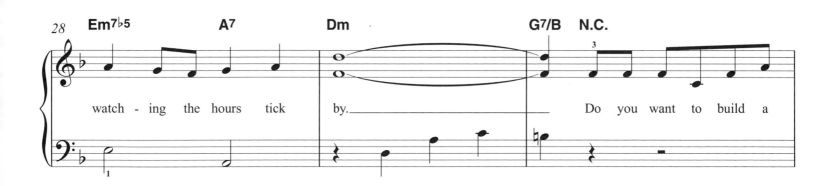

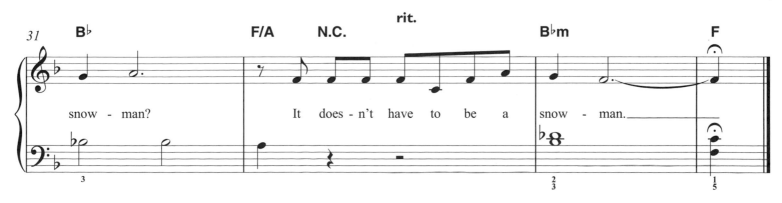

For the First Time in Forever

Music and Lyrics by Kristen Anderson-Lopez and Robert Lopez

Boasting excellent vocals from Kristen Bell (Anna) and Idina Menzel (Elsa), "For the First Time in Forever" tells the story of Anna's excitement when the gates are finally opened for Elsa's coronation. Elsa's part is a wonderful counterpoint melody that tells of her fear over accidentally revealing her powers. Filled with both seriousness and humor, the song features a line written by the writers' daughter: "I wanna stuff some chocolate in my face."

Hints & Tips: Play through any difficult-looking rhythms before you begin, making sure you count carefully. Look out for the 2/4 bar towards the end.

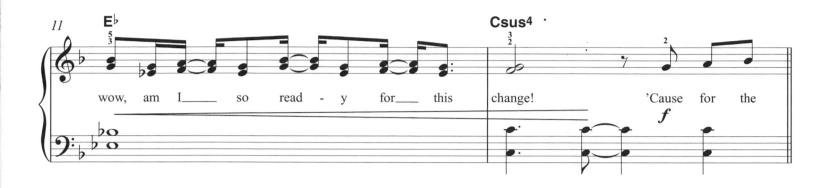

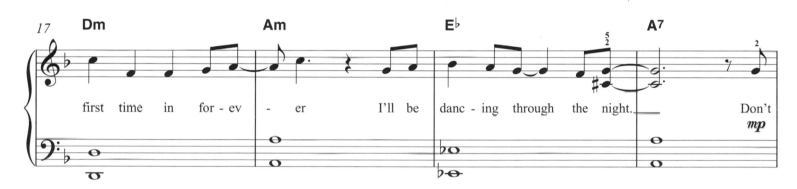

Fixer Upper

Music and Lyrics by Kristen Anderson-Lopez and Robert Lopez

After Anna is struck by Elsa's magic when she visits her sister's ice palace, Kristoff rushes her to his troll "family"
to try and cure her, but before he can explain her predicament to them, the trolls start singing this tune to try
to help the pair realize their feelings for each other. They tell Anna that Kristoff is a "fixer upper" — someone
who is a little rough around the edges, but ultimately very lovable. Whilst the song carries on, the trolls are
dressing the pair up in preparation for a marriage ceremony before Anna faints as her condition worsens.

Hints & Tips: Notice the way the tune passes from one hand to the other on the first page —
you can try to make each phrase sound like a different voice. Careful when choosing your tempo;
if you take it too fast, the repeated sixteenth notes will be too difficult. Keep this light and free.

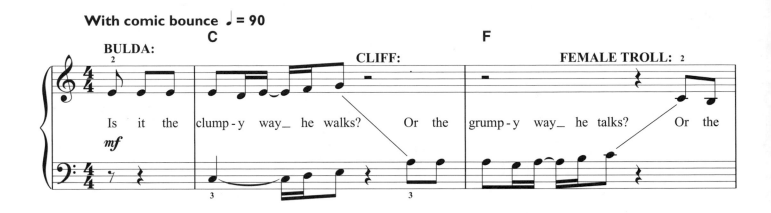

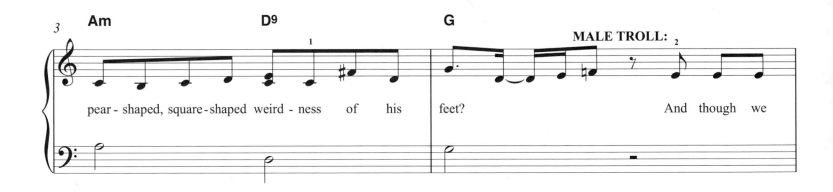

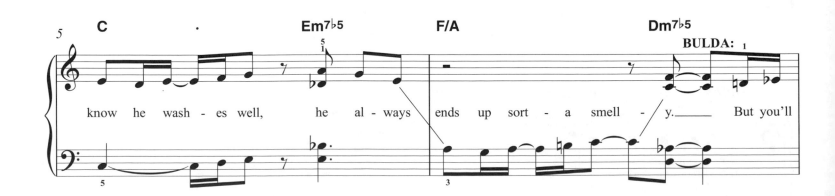

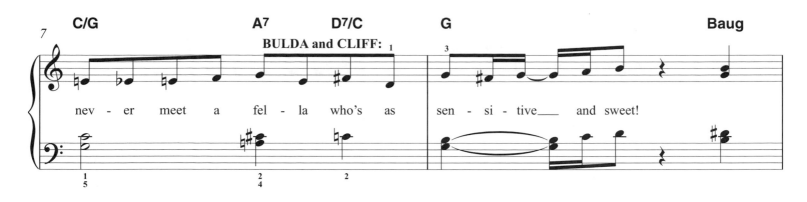

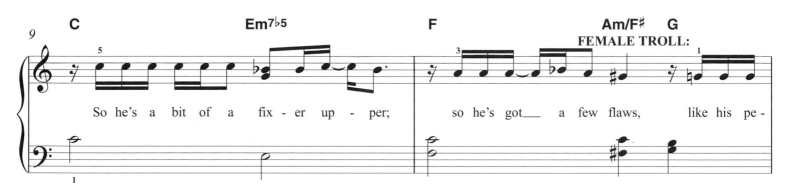

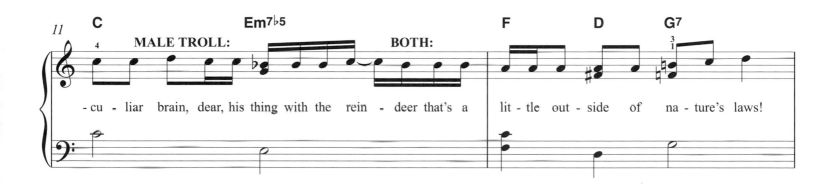

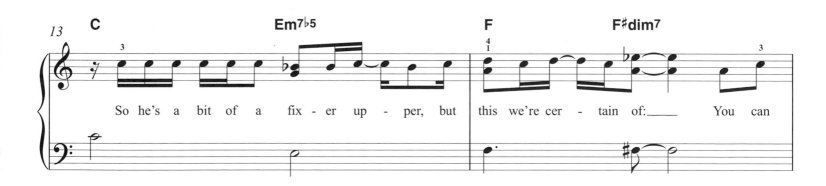

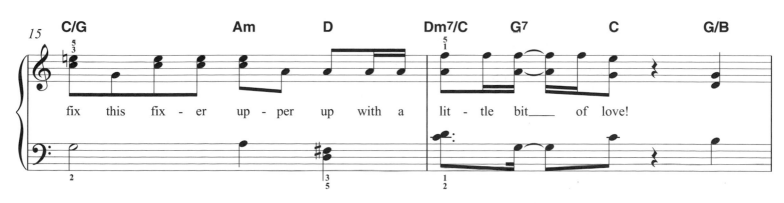

13

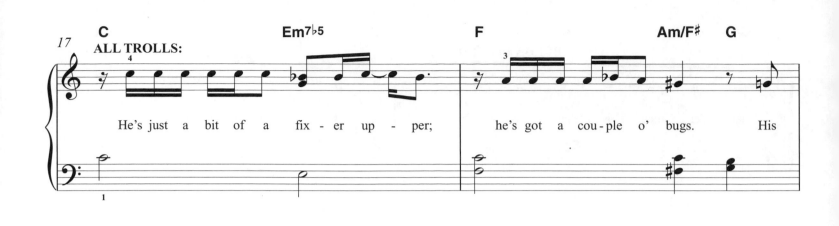

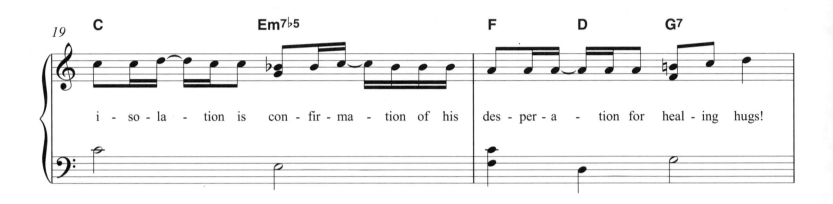

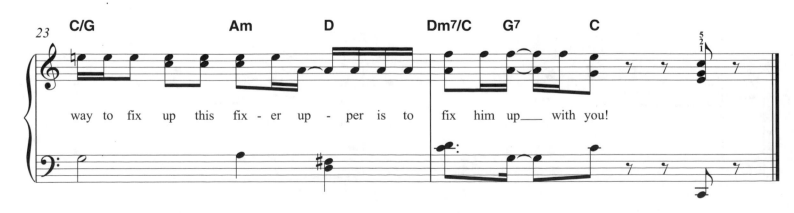

In Summer

Music and Lyrics by Kristen Anderson-Lopez and Robert Lopez

On their journey to find Elsa in order to stop the eternal winter, Anna and ice harvester, Kristoff, encounter an endearing snowman named Olaf, who is equally excited about the prospect of warm summer days and promptly breaks into song. Olaf sings to the pair about sunbathing and swimming while they listen in bewilderment, knowing that their new friend wouldn't last long in the heat! All three then continue on the journey, with Olaf leading them to Elsa.

Hints & Tips: Start by playing through the right hand on its own. There is quite a lot of detail in the melody line as the lyrics are quite busy. Careful when triplets combine with the swung eighth notes; listening to the song will help you understand the rhythm. Ultimately the song should sound carefree.

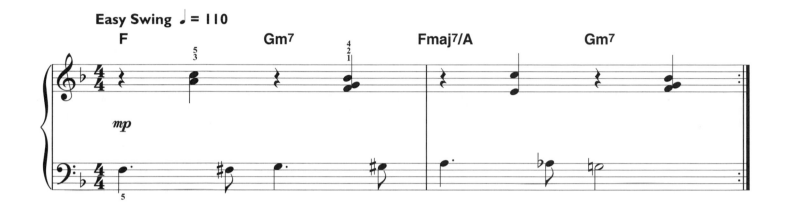

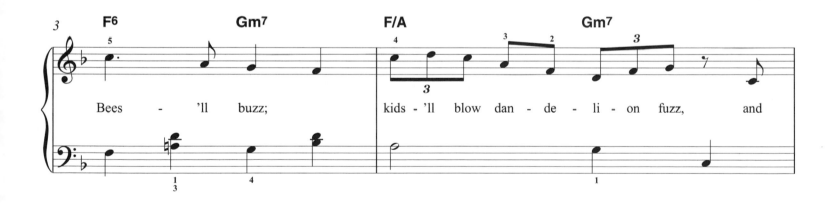

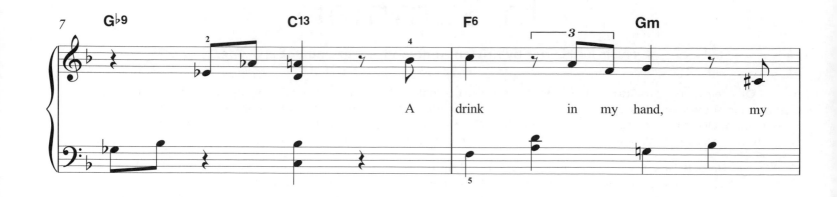

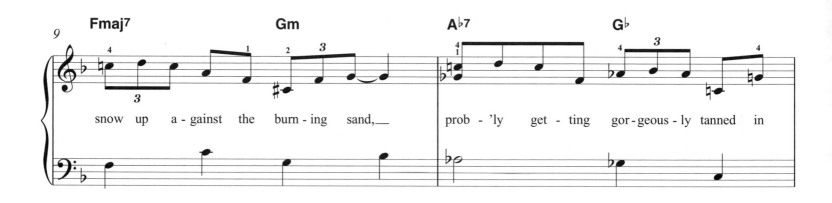

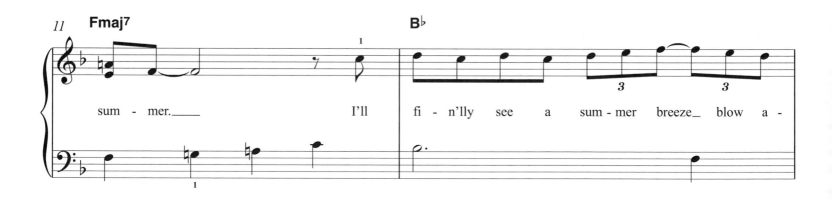

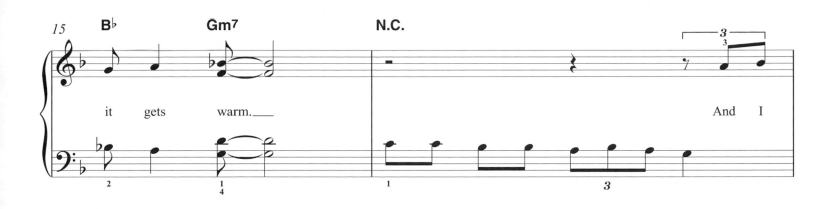

it gets warm.___ And I

can't wait to see what my bud - dies all think of me. Just im -

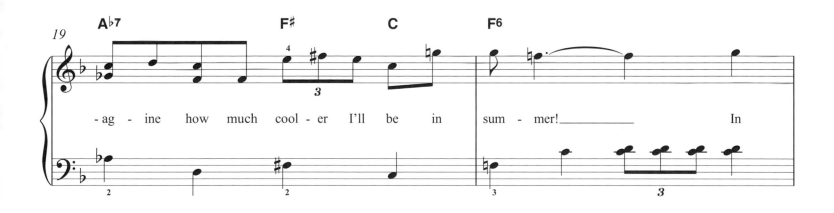

-ag - ine how much cool - er I'll be in sum - mer!_____ In

sum - mer!_____

Let It Go

Music and Lyrics by Kristen Anderson-Lopez and Robert Lopez

"Let It Go" has since become one of the best-selling singles of all time and has earned many accolades, including the Academy Award® for Best Original Song at the 86th Academy Awards. Composed by husband and wife songwriters Kristen Anderson-Lopez and Robert Lopez, the song was written for and originally performed by Idina Menzel, whose powerful vocals perfectly voiced Elsa's newfound freedom in the film. The song was reportedly composed in just a single day, after an inspiring walk in New York's Prospect Park.

Hints & Tips: There's a lot to watch out for in this, so look through and mark in pencil anything you're unsure of. Practice these bits thoroughly before putting the whole piece together.

Don't let__ them in,__ don't let__ them see,__ be the good girl you al-ways have_ to be,_

__con-ceal,_ don't feel,_ don't let__ them know,__ well, now__ they know._ Let it go,_

__ let it go,__ can't hold it back an-y-more._ Let it go,_

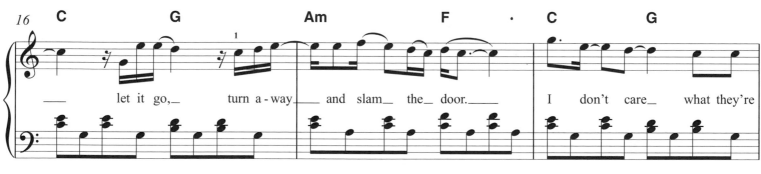

__ let it go,_ turn a-way__ and slam_ the_ door.__ I don't care_ what they're

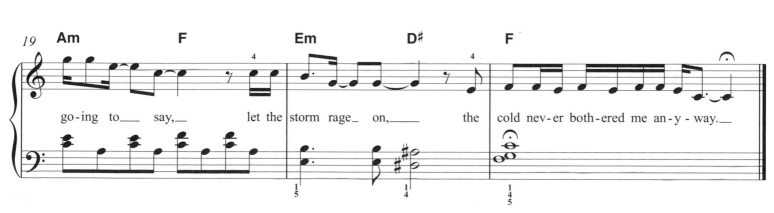

go-ing to__ say,_ let the storm rage_ on,___ the cold nev-er both-ered me an-y-way.__

Love Is an Open Door

Music and Lyrics by Kristen Anderson-Lopez and Robert Lopez

This upbeat, uplifting track is sung as a duet between main character Anna and her new love interest, Hans, whom she meets on the day of her sister Elsa's coronation. It's a whirlwind romance and "Love Is an Open Door" shows the couple's enthusiasm in finding each other, commenting on their "mental synchronization" and how they finish each other's "sandwiches"! At the end of the song, Hans proposes to Anna, who excitedly accepts.

Hints & Tips: Try and keep the right-hand eighth notes flowing evenly in some of the long phrases, like the first line. Bar 4 can be quieter, as this is just the accompaniment. When you get to the chorus the left hand can really drive the music forward. Play this louder.

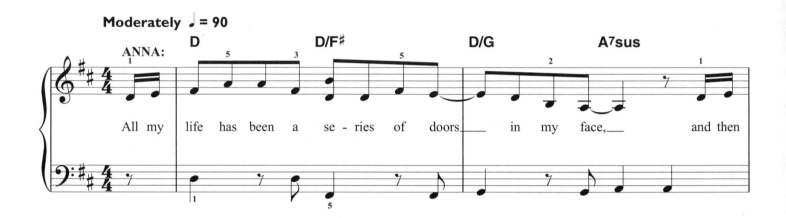

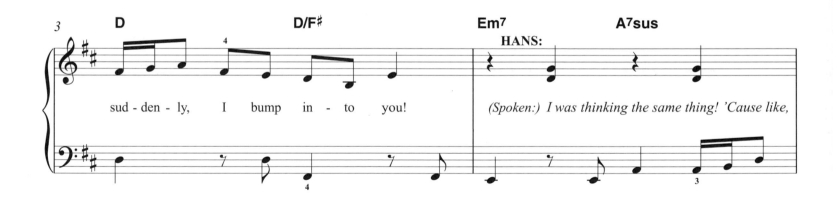

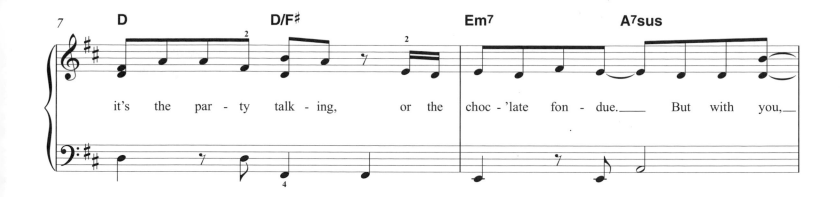

it's the par - ty talk - ing, or the choc - 'late fon - due.___ But with you,___

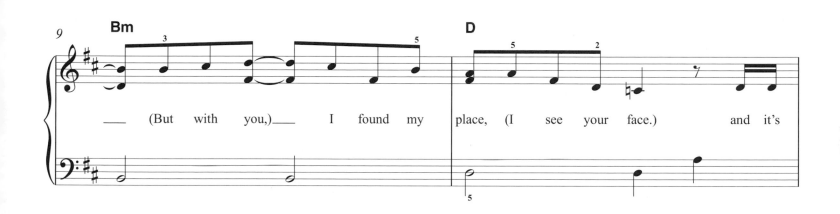

___ (But with you,)___ I found my place, (I see your face.) and it's

noth - ing like___ I've ev - er known___ be - fore. Love is an o - pen

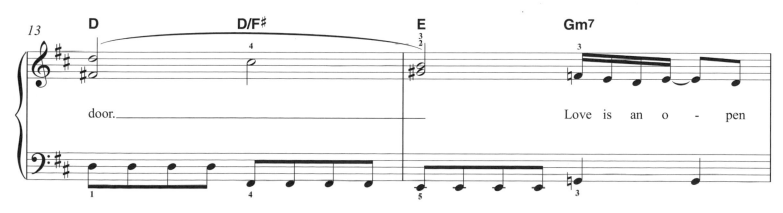

door.___ Love is an o - pen

Reindeer(s) Are Better Than People

Music and Lyrics by Kristen Anderson-Lopez and Robert Lopez

Kristoff sings this short and sweet tune to his reindeer, Sven, as they tuck up for the night. Comically, he sings it in such a way that it sounds like a duet between him and Sven, with Kristoff impersonating what his reindeer's voice would sound like. They then settle into sleep before Anna emphatically throws the stable door open to ask Kristoff to take her on a journey to the North Mountain to find Elsa, and stop the winter.

Hints & Tips: This song should sound very free, like an improvisation. Sing or say the words to yourself; then try and play in the same conversational way. Check the key signature: two sharps.

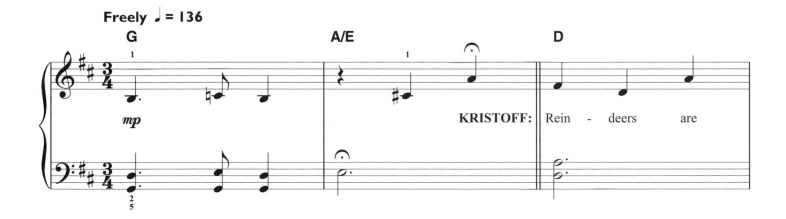

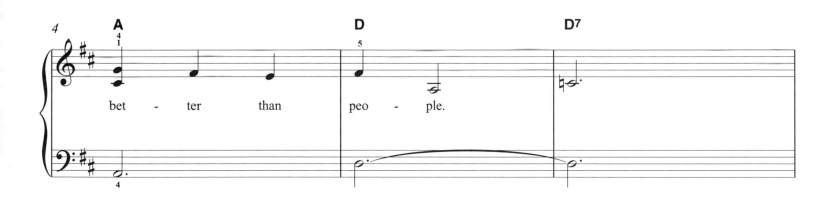

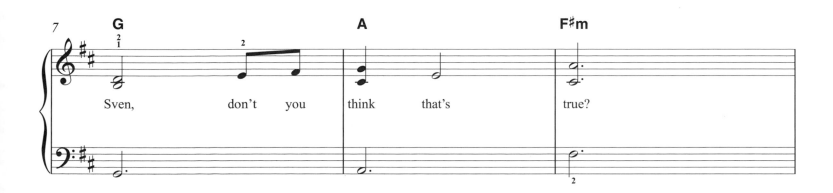

KRISTOFF (as Sven): Yeah, peo - ple will beat you and
curse you and cheat you. Ev - 'ry one of 'em's
bad, ex - cept you. **KRISTOFF:** *Aww, thanks buddy!* But
peo - ple smell bet - ter than rein - deers.

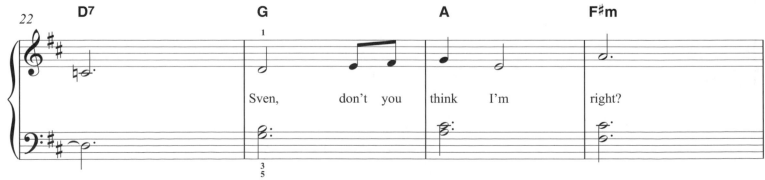

Sven, don't you think I'm right?

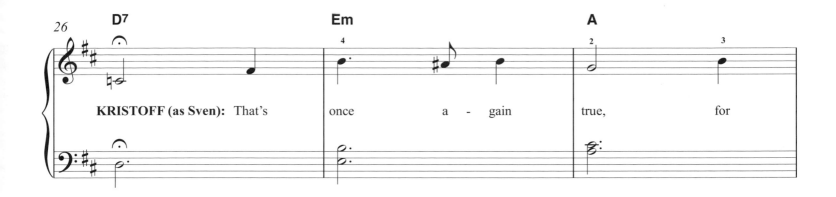

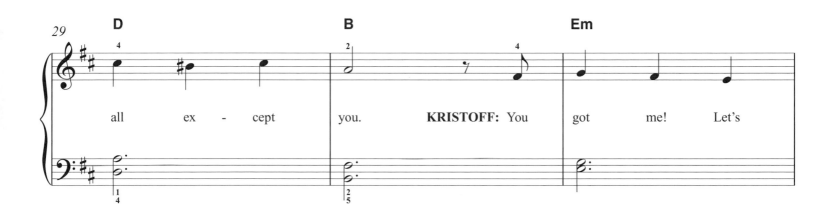

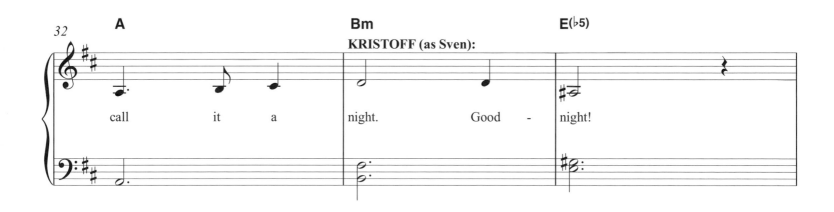

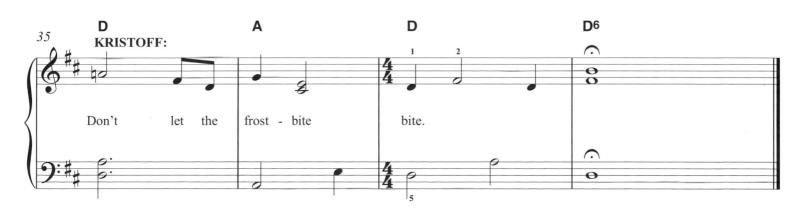

FROZEN II

All Is Found

Music and Lyrics by Kristen Anderson-Lopez and Robert Lopez

This is the first song we hear in *Frozen 2* when we see a flashback to Anna and Elsa as children with their parents, King Agnarr and Queen Iduna. It is their mother — voiced by Evan Rachel Wood — who sings this lullaby to them, which the pair reprise whenever they need to feel comforted. Hidden in the lyrics are clues to what lies ahead for Anna and Elsa, who embark on a voyage together to discover the story behind Elsa's powers.

Hints & tips: Try to hold down both left-hand notes in the first two bars. Same with the end of the song. There are no sharps or flats for most of the first two pages, but in the third we change key; watch out for F♯ and C♯ here.

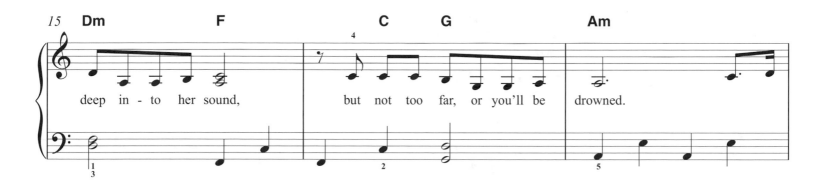

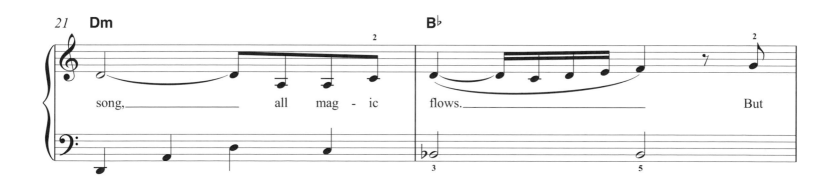

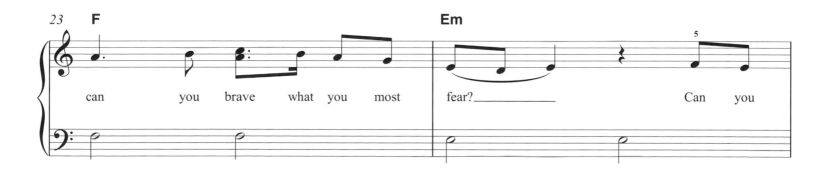

face   what the riv - er knows?   Where the

north wind_____ meets the   sea,   there's a   moth - er_____ full of

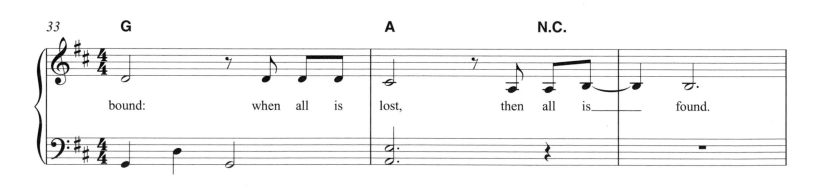

mem - o - ry.   Come,   my   darl - ing,   home - ward

bound: when all   is   lost,   then all   is____   found.

Into the Unknown

Music and Lyrics by Kristen Anderson-Lopez and Robert Lopez

We follow Elsa's footsteps to discover more about her powers in *Frozen 2*, with "Into the Unknown" playing a central role in the movie's storyline. Questioning the meaning of her "secret siren", Elsa sings this tune to the disembodied voice that keeps her awake, luring her to follow its call. It's another epic journey for Elsa in this second film, accompanied by Anna, Kristoff, Sven and Olaf.

Hints & tips: Try to feel the dotted quarter note pulse of this song. A quick listen should help with the rhythm of the 'Ah's at the beginning. The left hand really drives the song forward from bar 33: it can be more insistent here. At the end the music goes back into its shell, with an echo of the beginning.

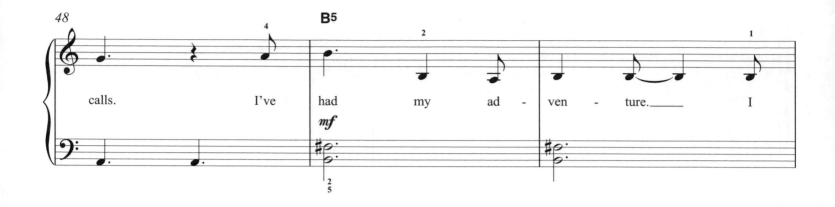

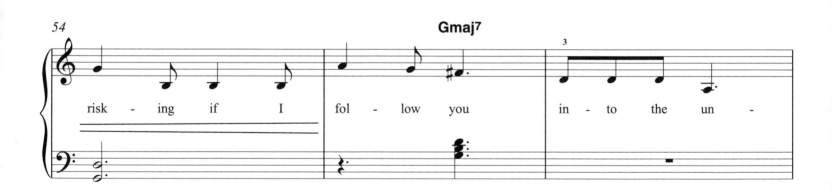

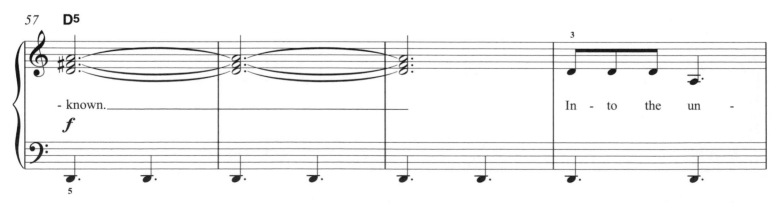

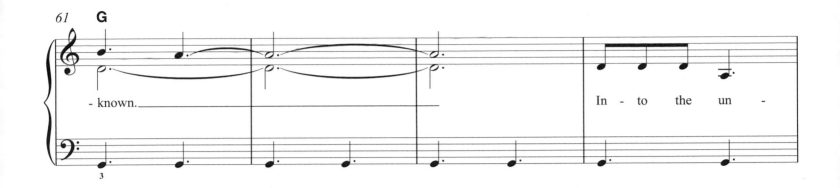

known.

Into the un -

known!

(Ah,

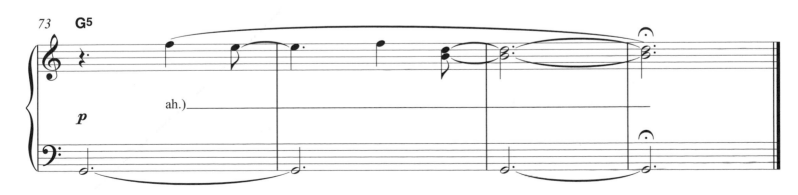

ah.)

35

Lost in the Woods

Music and Lyrics by Kristen Anderson-Lopez and Robert Lopez

Having only had one solo song with the brief serenade, "Reindeer(s) Are Better Than People", to Sven in *Frozen*, Kristoff — voiced by Jonathan Groff — flexes his vocal cords a little more in this sequel with "Lost in the Woods". After Anna leaves him behind to search for Elsa, Kristoff realizes how much he loves her, singing about how he is lost without her and things don't make sense unless she's around. The song is an 80s power ballad parody, complete with Sven and other reindeer providing backing vocals as Kristoff sings his heart out on screen.

Hints & tips: Take note of the key signatures in this song: G major in the verse and B♭ major in the chorus. There are a few places where both hands play a chord on the last beat of a bar, eg. bars 11, 25 and 27. You could give these beats a slight accent.

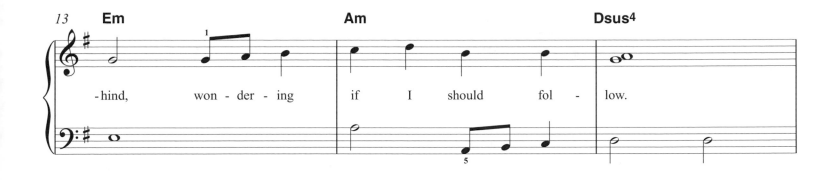

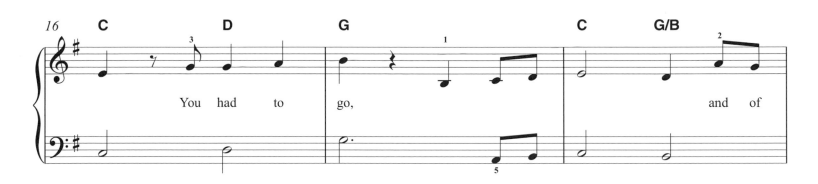

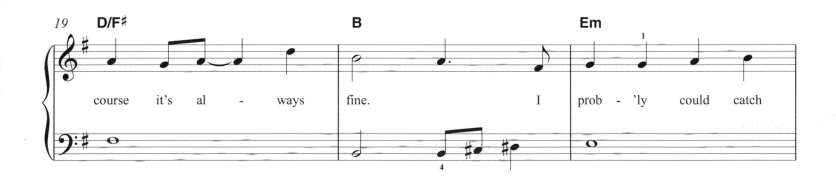

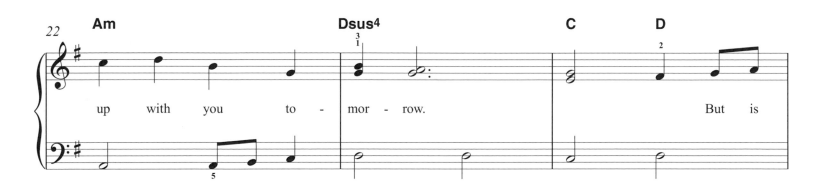

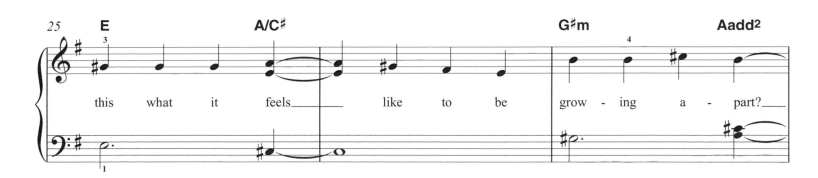

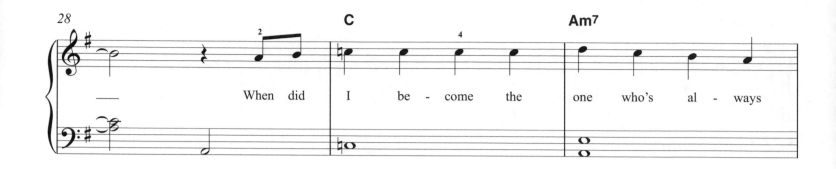

When did I be - come the one who's al - ways

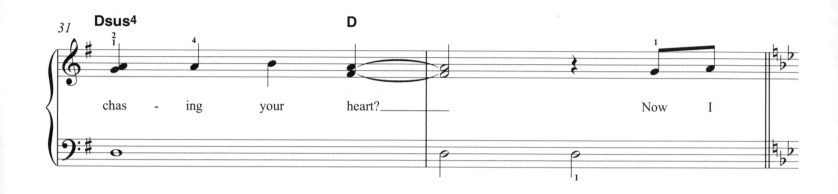

chas - ing your heart? Now I

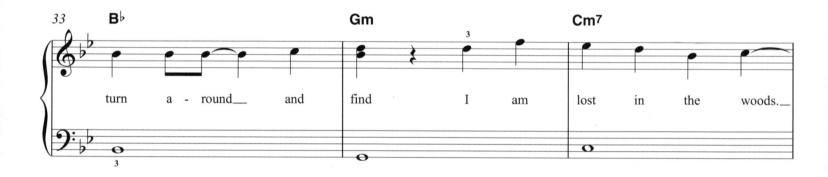

turn a - round and find I am lost in the woods.

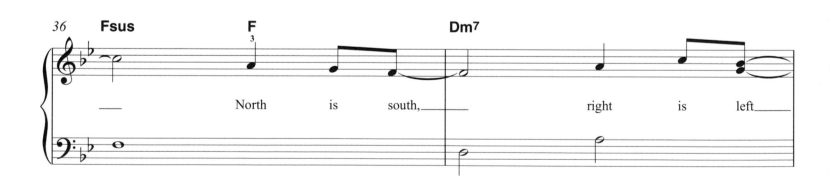

North is south, right is left

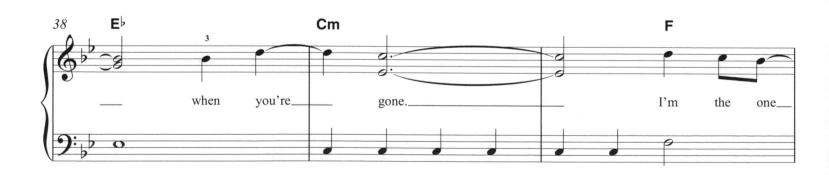

when you're gone. I'm the one

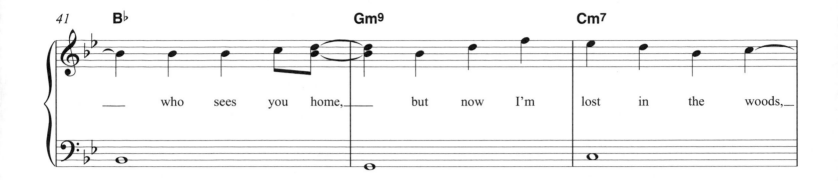

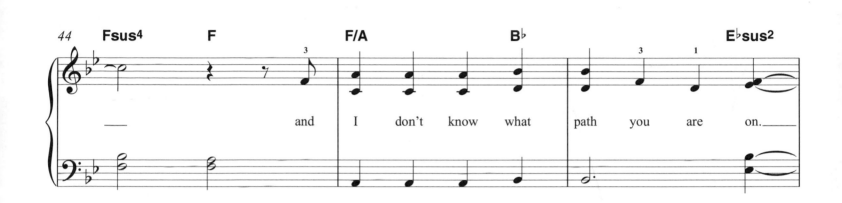

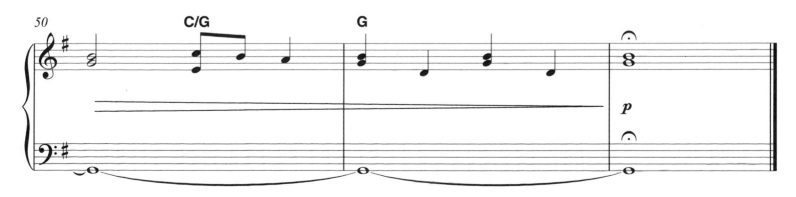

The Next Right Thing

Music and Lyrics by Kristen Anderson-Lopez and Robert Lopez

Towards the end of *Frozen 2* comes this haunting song from Anna, who is consumed by grief but determined to carry on and rise above it. In "The Next Right Thing", Anna sings about being in "darkness" and "stumbling blindly" towards the light in order to take the next step on her mission. Kristen Bell voices Anna in both *Frozen* films, including all her songs, as the actress has a background in classical music and musical theater!

Hints & tips: The beginning of this one should feel very free: don't worry too much about the exact rhythms in the right hand, just keep it natural. Try and maintain the soft dynamic throughout.

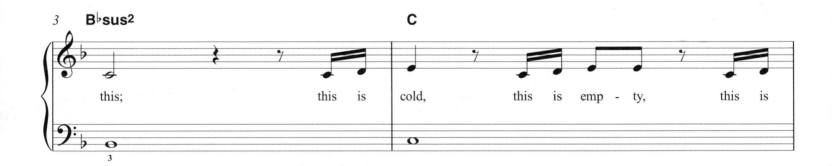

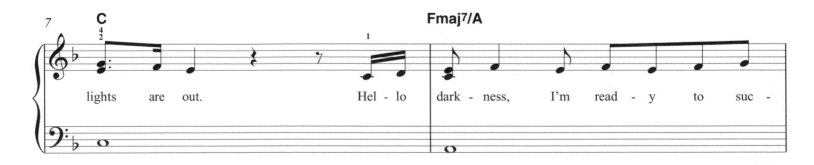

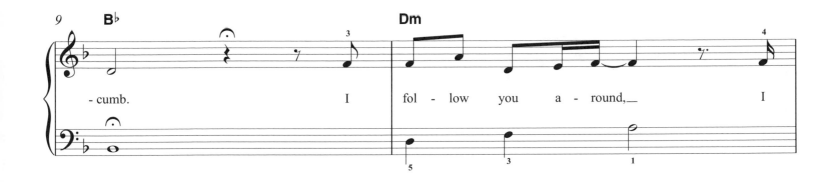

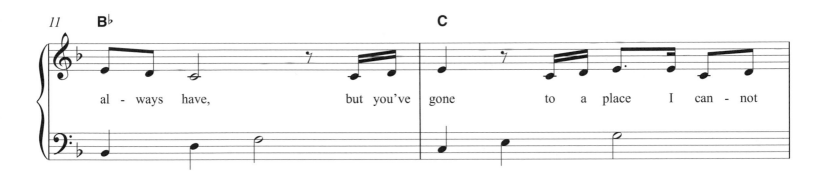

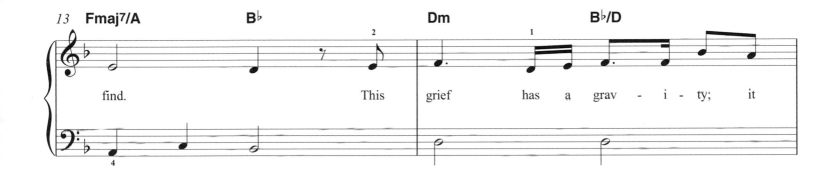

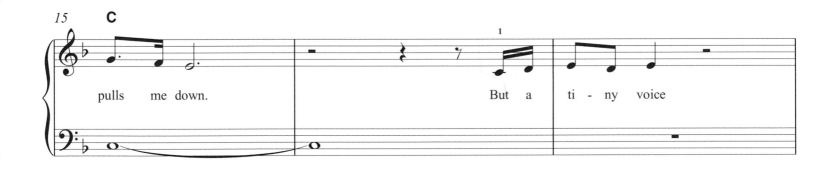

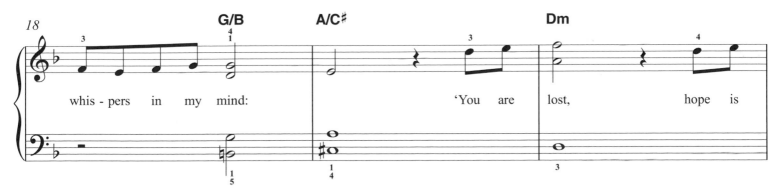

gone,   but you must   go on   and

do the next right thing.'

Steadily

Can there be a day be - yond this

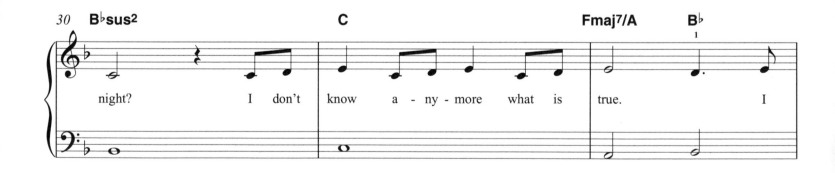

night? I don't know a - ny - more what is true.   I

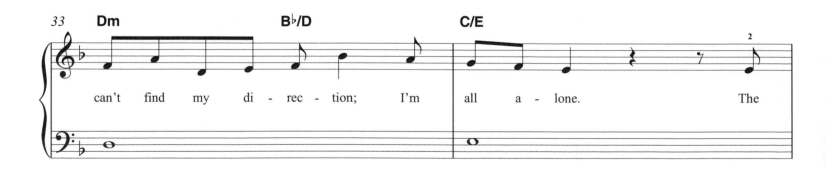

can't find my di - rec - tion; I'm all a - lone.   The

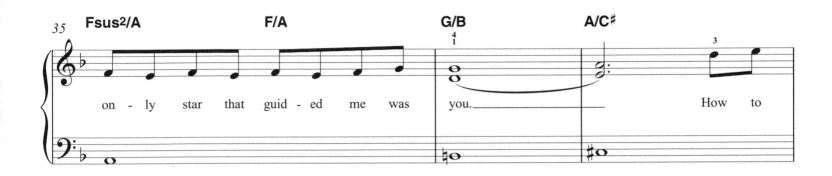

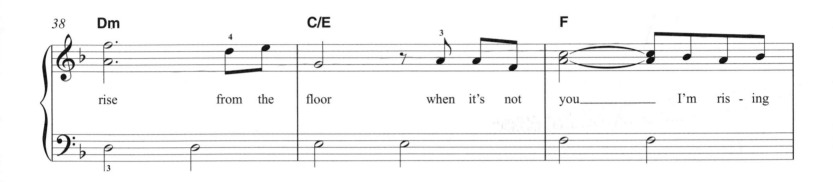

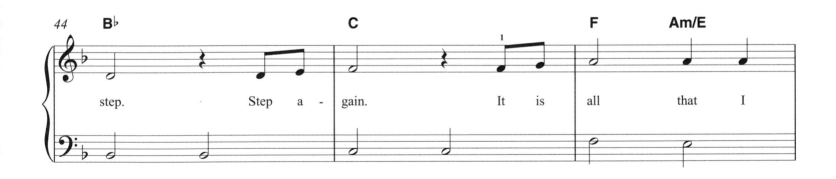

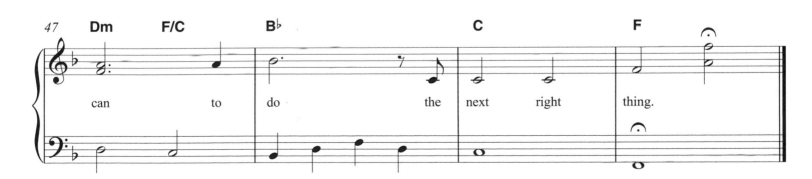

Show Yourself

Music and Lyrics by Kristen Anderson-Lopez and Robert Lopez

Sung by actresses Idina Menzel and Evan Rachel Wood, who play Elsa and Queen Iduna respectively, "Show Yourself"
accompanies the moment Elsa finally has her questions answered in the film. Having spent years wondering why she
was born with magic, Elsa comes to understand her true purpose, with the help of the memory of her mother,
who duets with her in this spine-tingling song about standing up and facing challenges head on.

Hints & tips: This is in an easy key, but just be careful of the flats you have to play in bars 27—29.
Most of the right-hand rhythm is fairly instinctive; just make note of the quarter note triplets.
There are several of these, and they should sound natural and unhurried.

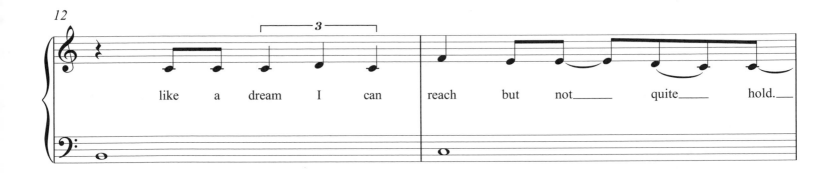

like a dream I can reach but not_____ quite_____ hold.___

___ I can sense you there,___ like a friend I've al -

-ways known._____ I'm ar - riv - ing,

and it feels like I am home._____ I have

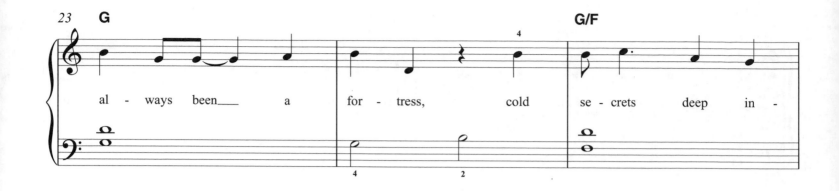

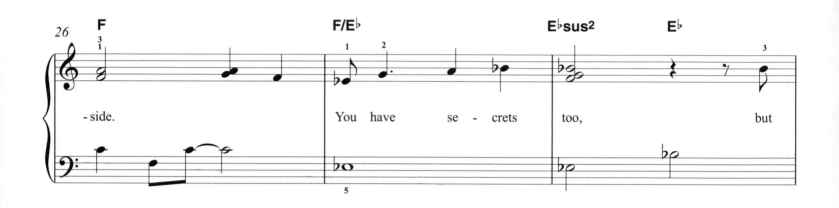

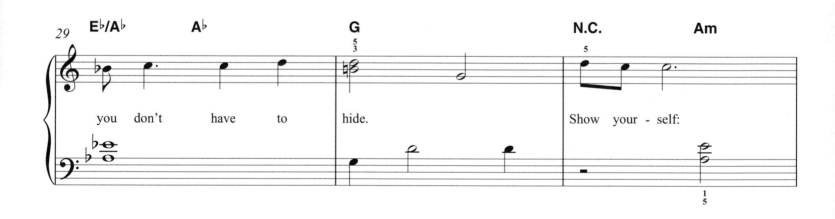

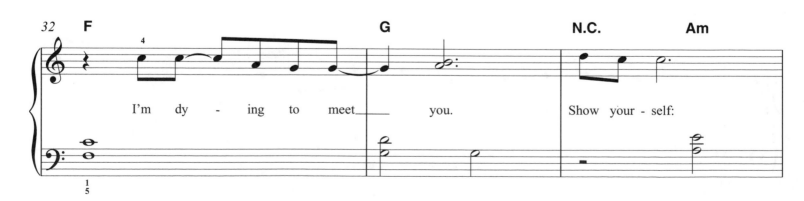

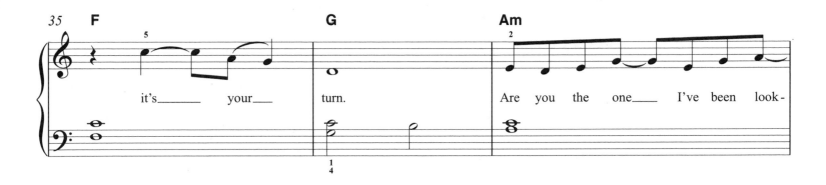

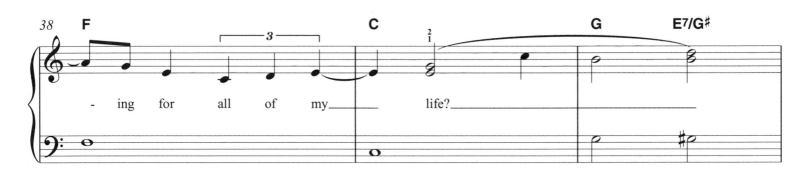

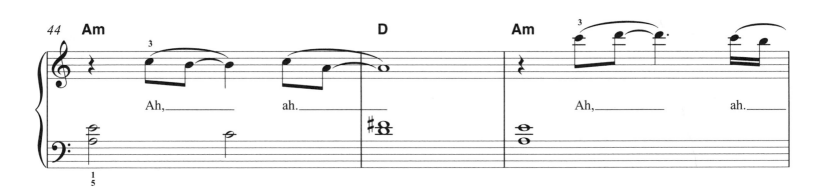

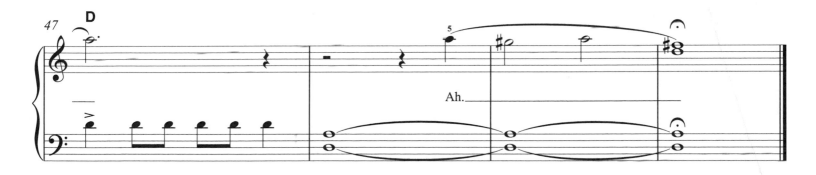

Some Things Never Change

Music and Lyrics by Kristen Anderson-Lopez and Robert Lopez

"Some Things Never Change" serves as a catch up with each character for the audience, as *Frozen 2* is set three years after the events of the first film. We can see that Anna and Kristoff are still very much in love, with Sven the reindeer remaining loyal to Kristoff, while Olaf is loving life in the kingdom and Elsa treasures each moment, but is wary of changes that seem to be on the horizon for the group.

Hints & tips: Position your left hand so that your 4th finger covers the B♭. Play this line through a few times on its own before adding the right hand. Try a slower tempo at first, as the repeated right-hand sixteenth notes will take a bit of getting used to.

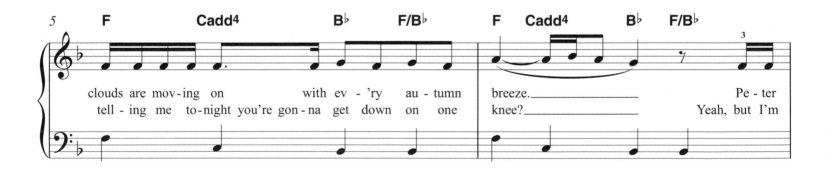

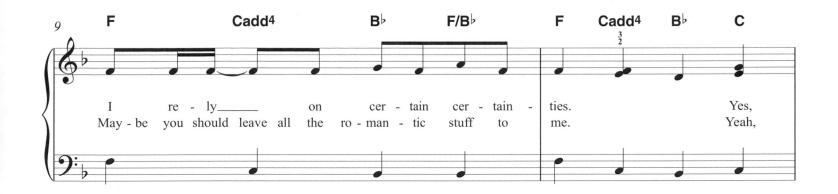

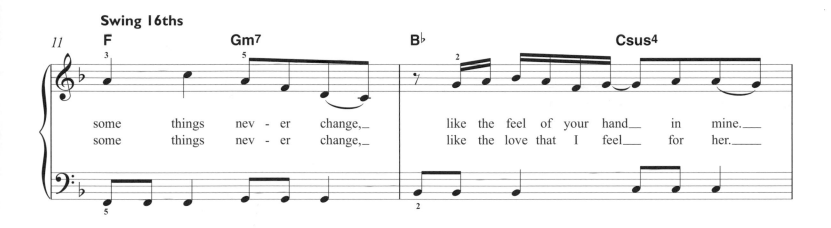

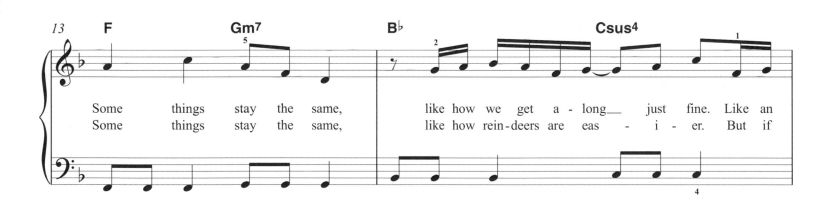

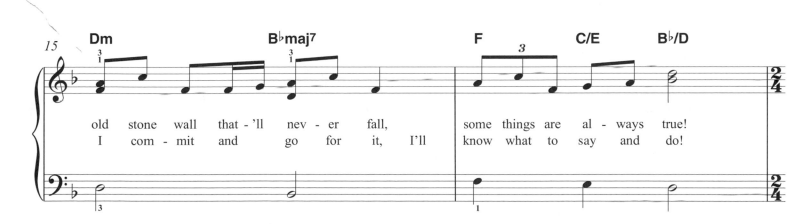

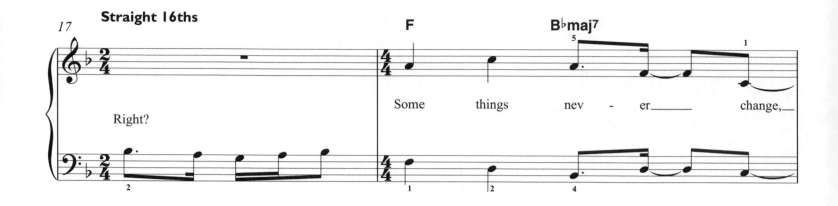

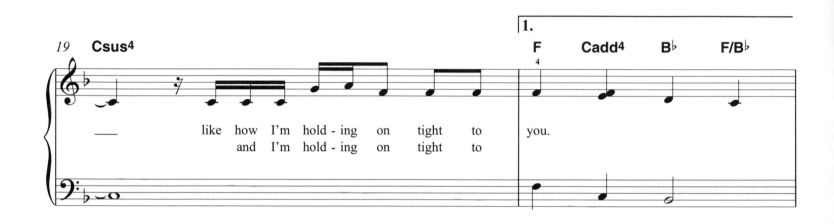

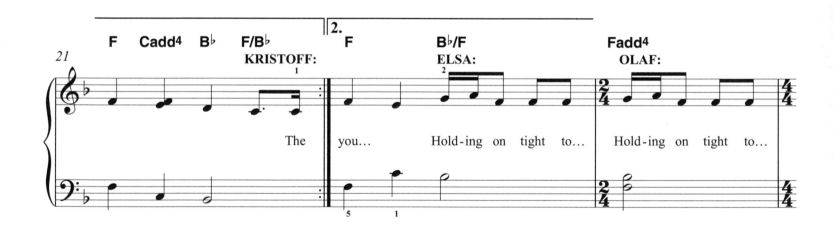

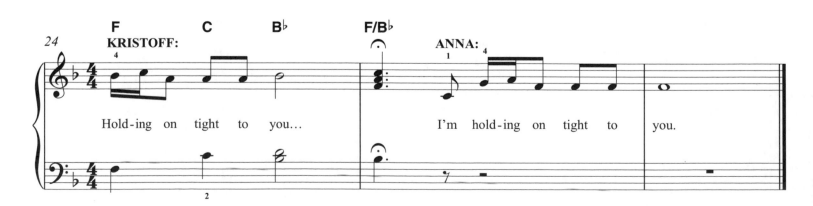

When I Am Older

Music and Lyrics by Kristen Anderson-Lopez and Robert Lopez

Olaf — voiced by Josh Gad — sings this charming short song to soothe his fears when he becomes separated from the group in the Enchanted Forest and finds himself at the mercy of the elemental spirits. Meanwhile, Olaf tries very hard to maintain a sunny disposition, telling himself he'll understand all these events when he's older and wiser, and he'll be rid of his "childish fears".

Hints & tips: This song has a lot of character, with lots of sudden accents and loud chords which you can enjoy. If you get the swing rhythm right, the triplets will be straightfoward. Try and keep the left hand *staccato*, although the contrast with the right hand articulation may be tricky.

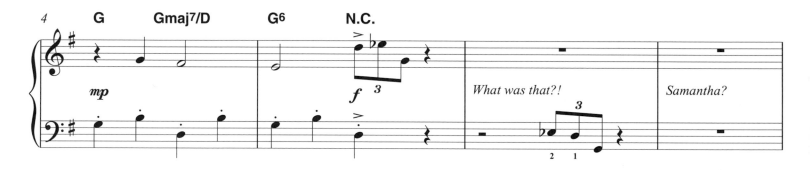

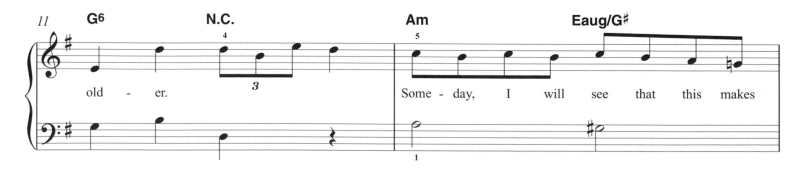

that will all make sense when I am old - er, so there's

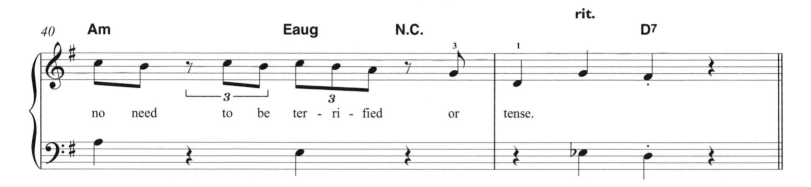

no need to be ter - ri - fied or tense.

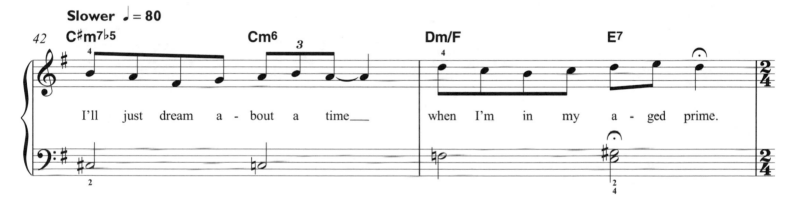

I'll just dream a - bout a time___ when I'm in my a - ged prime.

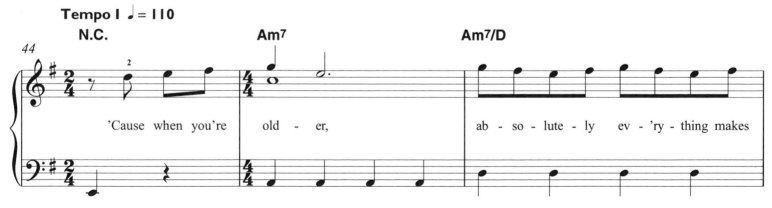

'Cause when you're old - er, ab - so - lute - ly ev - 'ry - thing makes

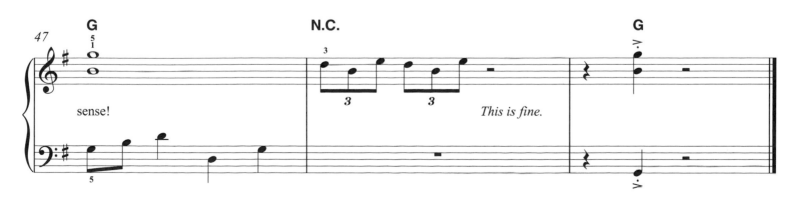

sense! *This is fine.*

Discover the rest of our *Really Easy Piano: Disney* volumes

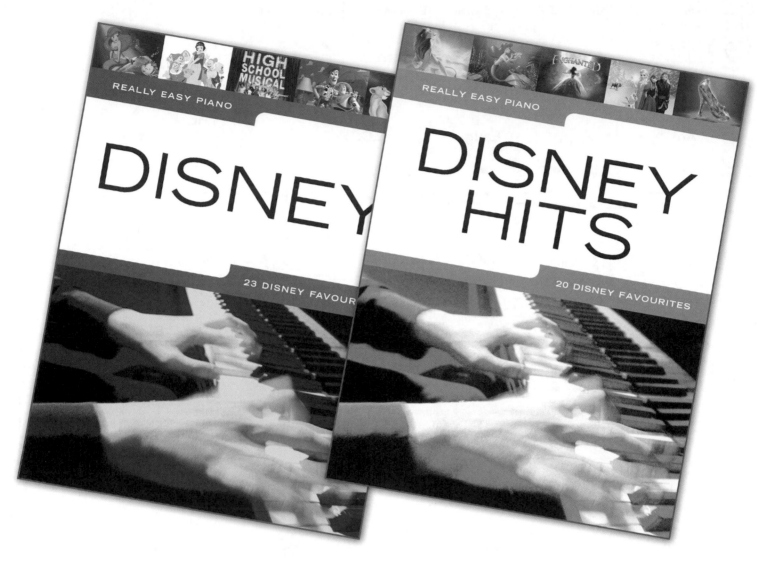

HL00311916

A Whole New World - Baby Mine - Beauty and the Beast - Bibbidi-Bobbidi-Boo - Breaking Free - Can You Feel the Love Tonight - Candle on the Water - Chim Chim Cher-ee - Colors of the Wind - Happy Working Song - If I Didn't Have You - Little April Shower - Someone's Waiting for You - The Bare Necessities - The Climb - Under the Sea - When She Loved Me - When You Wish Upon a Star - Whistle While You Work - You'll Be in My Heart - You've Got a Friend in Me - Zero to Hero - Zip-a-Dee-Doo-Dah

HL00154998

A Dream Is a Wish Your Heart Makes - Almost There - Be Our Guest - Shut Up and Drive - Strong - That's How You Know - Touch the Sky - We Belong Together - Bundle of Joy - Down to Earth - For the First Time in Forever - I Just Can't Wait to Be King - I See the Light - I Thought I Lost You - Immortals - Lava - Let It Go - Once Upon a Dream - Part of Your World - Reflection

Just visit your local music shop and ask to see our huge range of music in print,